PrecisionFaith Prayer Series

Jesus
21 Days That Can Change
The Way You Pray

Toby Lofton

Scripture quotations taken from The Holy Bible, New International Version® NIV® Copyright © 1973 1978 1984 2011 by Biblica, Inc. TM Used by permission. All rights reserved worldwide.

PrecisionFaith Prayer Series
Jesus:
21 Days That Can Change the Way You Pray

PrecisionFaith.com

Copyright © 2020 Toby Lofton

All rights reserved. No part of this publication may be reproduced, distributed, or transmitted in any form or by any means, including photocopying, recording, or other electronic or mechanical methods, without the prior written permission of the publisher, except in the case of brief quotations embodied in reviews and certain other non-commercial uses permitted by copyright law. Please direct your inquiries to info@precisionfaith.com.

ISBN: 9798621406608

DEDICATION

Dedicated to the Master – Jesus Christ

CONTENTS

	Introduction	i
	How to Use This Book	v
Day 1	The Place of Prayer	1
Day 2	Blessings	5
Day 3	Revealing Prayer	8
Day 4	Praying God's Will	11
Day 5	Don't Leave Me	13
Day 6	May You Not Fail	16
Day 7	Strengthen Your Brothers	19
	PrecisionFaith Break	21
Day 8	Forgive Them	23
Day 9	I Give Myself to You	26
Day 10	Thanks for Listening	28
Day 11	Sent	32
	PrecisionFaith Break	35
Day 12	The Longest Prayer	37
Day 13	A Place to Glorify You	40

Day 14	Give Me the Words	43
Day 15	Let Them Hear	46
Day 16	Protection	49
Day 17	Those Not Yet	52
Day 18	Make Us One	55
Day 19	A Look Back	58
	PrecisionFaith Break	60
Day 20	A Long Look Back	61
Day 21	One Final Prayer	64

INTRODUCTION

Let me ask you some questions. Do you think it makes sense that as disciples of Jesus that we should pray like Jesus? Would it be great to pray as he prayed? Would you like to learn to pray that way?

If you answered "Yes", then read on.

If you answered "No", keep reading anyway. It might be that by the time you complete these twenty-one days your response to praying with Jesus may change.

Regardless of your answer, I am betting that your idea about what it means to be a disciple of Jesus may change. And, if you are not a disciple of Jesus, I pray that you will want to be one. If you have ever wanted to do something with your life, I cannot think of anything better to do. So read on. Please, read on.

Jesus taught his disciples to count the cost before starting on a venture. So, let me tell you what to expect from learning to pray with Jesus.

Learning to pray with Jesus will likely challenge the way you currently pray. If you take the prayers of Jesus seriously, you will probably have to reevaluate your concept of discipleship. If you decide to pray as Jesus prayed, you may do so with a bit of fear in your throat. Praying with Jesus is profound - profoundly different than most prayers you have heard or even said.

Think about the prayers you currently pray. How do they typically go? What do they generally sound like?

Before I started praying with Jesus, my prayers went something like this:

> - Praising God just for being God.
> - Sometimes I asked for forgiveness or apologized for something I did.
> - I thanked him for his love and mercy; maybe for something I had received or attributed to God's goodness.
> - Then I usually asked him for a few more things, maybe guidance, maybe help for someone else.

Now, there is nothing wrong with such a prayer, but when I started looking at the prayers of Jesus, I quickly realized something was missing in my prayers. My prayers seemed kind of weak in comparison. I felt like I was missing something. In fact, I felt like I was short-changing God. I even asked myself, what have I been doing?

Think about your church. How do prayers generally go in your church?

As a pastor, I spend a lot of time in churches. When I think back about all the prayers I have spoken and heard in church, I also realize some discrepancies. My experience with prayers in church go something like this:

- Praising God and thanking God for a variety of things.
- Maybe something about forgiveness in a general way.
- Then we pray for everybody and their neighbor who is sick. We pray for people in the church that are sick. We pray for people who I have no idea who they are, but someone requested prayer on their behalf. We pray for the nation and any other significant global events. We pray for peace. You get the idea.

Once again, there is nothing wrong with such prayers, but when we start looking at the prayers of Jesus it becomes clearly obvious, we are negating something in our prayers. We are missing out on joining Jesus in asking for things from our Father that can totally change us, change others, change people we haven't even considered, and truly change the world.

It is my prayer that as you join me in looking at the prayers of Jesus that the way you pray will be changed for the rest of your life. I absolutely believe that it will. I believe it because it has mine. I pray that it will also take you, your church, and your pastor to an entirely different level of discipleship (you will understand later why I include your church and pastor). And, in a mind-blowing way, I pray that as a result of your prayers, the people who you lead to Christ and the people they lead to Christ will be changed (more on this later also).

You are about to embark on a prayer journey of a lifetime. It can change the way you pray for the rest of your life and draw you to a different place in your relationship with the Father, the Son, and the Holy Spirit.

Let's go.

How to Use This Book

This book is written as a daily devotional. Each day we will look at a different aspect of the prayers of Jesus. Each day will be different. However, some days will build on other days; especially as we get to the longest prayer that Jesus prayed that we have in the Bible.

Each day will begin with scripture references. In this devotional I used the New International Version (NIV).

Following the scriptures, I will provide some brief thoughts about the scripture and the context of which Jesus prayed. In these thoughts, I will discuss how to apply the prayers of Jesus to your life and context. I will consider what the prayer might look like if you said something similar. I will also expand the prayer to your church and to your pastor. The longest prayer particularly stretches the horizons of our prayers (more on that on those days).

Why do I include your church and pastor? I must give credit to Jim Maxim. Jim Maxim is the founder of ACTS413 Ministries. ACTS413 ministries focuses on intercessory prayer for pastors, their families, churches, cities, and nations. As a pastor, it was heartwarming to see such an emphasis placed on praying for men and women like me, our families, and the body of Christ. So I encourage you to pray for your pastor and church as you learn to pray with Jesus. The impact of praying these prayers for your pastor and church will become evident as we explore them.

At the end of each reflection upon the prayers of Jesus, I will provide a model prayer. I suggest one of two approaches with the model prayer. The first approach: pray it as it is. Make that prayer your prayer for the day. The second approach: let it be a template and modify it according to how you want to pray the prayer. Use caution, however. Ensure you are keeping with the primary themes Jesus provided in his prayers.

You will also find three PrecisionFaith Breaks in the book. These are not counted as part of the twenty-one days. The Breaks provide other approaches to praying with Jesus. They also address considerations that we may need to address in our prayer life and understanding of being a disciple.

Know that I am praying for you. Know that I join you in these prayers. This is exciting stuff and I am very excited about what God is going to do in your life.

DAY 1
THE PLACE OF PRAYER

"Very early in the morning, while it was still dark, Jesus got up, left the house and went off to a solitary place, where he prayed." Mark 1:35

"After leaving them, he went up on a mountainside to pray." Mark 6:46

"When all the people were being baptized, Jesus was baptized too. And as he was praying, heaven was opened..." Luke 3:21

"Once when Jesus was praying in private and his disciples were with him, he asked them, "Who do the crowds say I am?"" Luke 9:18

"About eight days after Jesus said this, he took Peter, John and James with him and went up onto a mountain to pray." Luke 9:28

> *"One day Jesus was praying in a certain place. When he finished, one of his disciples said to him, "Lord, teach us to pray, just as John taught his disciples.""* Luke 11:1

My wife and I were eating in a restaurant with my family. A man entered the restaurant and began talking with people he apparently knew. After his conversation, he found a seat at a table. He ordered his food and received his drink. When the waiter brought the man his food, he took off his cap, bowed his head, and began to pray. My wife elbowed me and pointed the man out as he was praying. This man wasn't just asking a blessing for his food. If he was, he was praying over every ingredient. It was obvious this man was praying for much more. I do not know what he was saying, but rarely have I witnessed such intense prayer over a meal.

Today we are considering six instances of the prayers of Jesus. In these prayers we do not know what he prayed. We only know that he prayed.

Jesus prayed in many places. Sometimes he prayed alone. Sometimes in a deserted place. Other times on a mountain. And, then there are places not defined. Yet he prayed. He prayed at his baptism. He prayed with three of his disciples. He prayed with the disciples and others nearby. But prayed he did. The point is that Jesus prayed. Where he prayed didn't seem to matter. Jesus was comfortable praying to his father anywhere.

Praying anywhere is often a challenge for many of us. We are uncomfortable praying in public, even when praying in silence. Many of us prefer the flash blessing at our meals. We know we should bless our food but are uncomfortable doing it. So, we do the millisecond prayer. You know, the one where you just close your eyes and bow really, really, quick. I've been guilty.

If we are going to pray with Jesus, we must become comfortable praying anywhere and in front of anyone. I am not talking about you leading a group in prayer. I get it. Some people are just too uncomfortable there. That said, if this is you, I pray that by the time you finish this book you will overcome that fear. Not because you have mustered up enough courage, but because by the time you finish this book you will have learned to pray with Jesus. You will know exactly what to pray and how to pray it. I pray that you will have such confidence in your relationship with God you will jump at every chance to pray before others. In fact, by the end of this book, you will be asking God for such confidence in prayer. Pray we must though.

Today, and tomorrow, is going to be a bit different. Today you are receiving your marching orders. To really benefit from learning to pray with Jesus, you will need to venture into your community for these devotions if you are able. No, it is not a requirement. You can pray these devotions in your home or wherever you are comfortable. I would rather you be where you will pray than somewhere you will not. I still believe God can change the way you pray. But, if you really want to expand your prayer life, get outside in your community. Open this guidebook. Read the daily devotion. Then, right then, right there, pray the prayers. Don't be bashful. Don't worry about who sees you. You never know. Your act of faith may totally change another's prayer practice or even their life.

You may want to invite others to pray with you, just as Jesus did (go figure that). Share your daily devotion with them and ask them to pray with you.

What is important is that you pray. Pray for yourself. Pray for your pastor. Pray for your church and the work of the church. Just pray.

PRAYER

Father, today I am asking for you to lead me to pray. Make prayer such a part of my daily habit. Help me to pray anywhere.

Be with my church. Transform us to be a people of prayer. Help us to pray privately, collectively, and cooperatively.

Father, I pray that my pastor will be a pastor of prayer. May the time spent with you influence the way our pastor leads us.

Amen.

DAY 2
BLESSINGS

"And he took the children in his arms, placed his hands on them and blessed them." Mark 10:16

"When he had led them out to the vicinity of Bethany, he lifted up his hands and blessed them." Luke 24:50

Thomas Bandy teaches the trans-formative power of blessing others even when they do not know that they are being blessed. He teaches the practice of going into various places in the community and praying for people that you see by asking God to bless those persons.

As one who has followed this practice, I have come to believe it is the person doing the blessing that is transformed more than anyone else. There is something about asking God to bless people you do not know. And, after you have been to the same places several times, your heart begins to love the people you see.

Imagine that: loving the people you see. Perhaps this is part of growing into the image of Christ. Christ, who loved all. Christ, who blessed others. I can only imagine the number of stories that we do not have of Jesus blessing people. It just seems to be the fabric of Jesus' life.

What if you made this part of your fabric? What if you made it a practice of blessing others everywhere you went? I'm not just talking about the "God bless you" salutation (although those are good also). Rather, I am talking about a genuine in-your-face blessing. Oh, you don't have to speak it aloud to them - although that might be awesome. I am talking about lifting your heart to God and asking him to pour blessing upon blessing upon someone.

Perhaps if we started looking at others with a blessing as opposed to distrust, scrutiny, and judgment, we might begin to see with the eyes of God. Perhaps we will draw closer to praying like Jesus.

Pray blessings rather than dwelling upon differences, dislikes, and personal opinions. Paul taught to dwell on that which was good (Philippians 4:8). Blessings are good. Imagine if most of your time in prayer was spent on blessing others. Blessing God. Blessing your pastor. Blessing your church.

Today's prayer assignment is simple: Go to a place in your community, perhaps as a trial run for future prayer times, and simply pray blessings upon the people that are there. Pray for them one by one. Don't forget, pray blessings upon your pastor and your church while you are at it.

PRAYER

Father, I pray blessings upon my community. I ask that you pour your grace upon in it.

Bless my church in such a profound way that it will be undeniable that we have been blessed by you. As the Psalmist asked, so I ask, let others look upon us and know that we are your people.

Bless my pastor. Bless his ministry. Bless his family. Bless him as he leads us.

In the name of Jesus, Amen.

DAY 3
REVEALING PRAYER

"At that time Jesus said, "I praise you, Father, Lord of heaven and earth, because you have hidden these things from the wise and learned, and revealed them to little children. Yes, Father, for this is what you were pleased to do. "All things have been committed to me by my Father. No one knows the Son except the Father, and no one knows the Father except the Son and those to whom the Son chooses to reveal him. "Come to me, all you who are weary and burdened, and I will give you rest. Take my yoke upon you and learn from me, for I am gentle and humble in heart, and you will find rest for your souls. For my yoke is easy and my burden is light.""" Matthew 11:25-30.

Today we begin looking at the actual prayers of Jesus. Did you realize that only those whom Jesus chose to reveal God to got to know God? According to this prayer of Jesus, God hid the truth, eternal life, from those who God knew wouldn't receive that truth. It is like God knows who will and who will not have a receiving heart. God knows who will listen and who will not. (This will be important for us to understand when we get to *The Longest Prayer* section.)

Guess what this means if you are a disciple of Jesus? God has revealed himself to you through his son. You can say to God, "Thank you for revealing yourself to me." Sometimes I wonder if we lose sight of that great truth. Sometimes we get so caught up in life that we forget the incredible truth that God showed himself to us. If you pause and think of the magnitude of that, it can shake your soul.

As a church leader, I have been in meetings where I only wished we would stop our debating and spend time on this great truth. Can you imagine what might happen during times of tension if the church would stop and pray:

"Father, we thank you for revealing yourself to us. You didn't have to, but you did. You could have left us to ourselves, much like we are acting right now. But you didn't. You revealed yourself to us and made us yours. You made us one with each other."

Makes me wonder how our conversations would follow if we did.

Know this: If you believe in your heart and confess with your mouth that Jesus is Lord, you are a child of God. The reason you are God's child is because God chose to reveal himself to you through his Son. You did not come to this understanding by your own power or might. God did it. So, be thankful.

PRAYER

I thank you Father, Lord of heaven and earth, creator of everything I see, creator of me. I thank you for revealing yourself to me. I know you didn't have to, but you did. For this I am so grateful.

I thank you for revealing yourself to my Church – the people within it. Remind us daily that you loved us enough to show us yourself through Jesus.

I pray for my pastor also. In his work - the struggles, difficulties, and celebrations – make it known to him that you chose him. May he find strength for his ministry through this great truth as he proclaims that great call of Jesus, "Come to me, all you that are weary and are carrying heavy burdens, and I will give you rest."

DAY 4
PRAYING GOD'S WILL

"Going a little farther, he fell with his face to the ground and prayed, "My Father, if it is possible, may this cup be taken from me. Yet not as I will, but as you will."

"He went away a second time and prayed, "My Father, if it is not possible for this cup to be taken away unless I drink it, may your will be done."" Matthew 26:39, 42.

This is the prayer of Jesus the night before his arrest. He knew that he was going to be arrested and crucified. One can only imagine the anguish he felt knowing what was to come in the hours and days ahead.

This is certainly one of the prayers of Jesus that only he can pray. No other person can ever know or feel what Jesus was experiencing. He was about to bear the sins of the world – a burden reserved only for Jesus.

While we can't pray this prayer of Jesus, we can learn from two phrases:

"… not as I will, but as you will." and
"…your will be done."

This ought to be the heart of every prayer we pray. While we may ask for various things (and God wants us to ask), we must ask only according to his will. God's will is perfect. God's provisions are perfect. Often we may not know what that perfect will might be, but we can ask. We can ask for what we want and then pray that his will be done.

Regardless of what you are facing, what you are praying for, or what you are asking from our Father, imagine if today you were praying for his perfect will to be done.

PRAYER

Father, while I may have a lot on my mind, while I may have things I would like to ask, my number one prayer is for your will be done. Like Jesus, I may ask for something else, but in the end, it is what you want that matters. So, I am asking for that Lord. I am asking for your will for me.

I am asking for your will for my church. We have all sorts of ideas and thoughts about how we should do church. We have our own solutions to the issues we face. But, it is your will that matters most. May your will be done in our church.

I pray also that you will attune my pastor's ear to your will. Help him to know. Help him to see it. Let him not get his own dreams and vision in the path of your dreams and vision. Let your will be done.

DAY 5
DON'T LEAVE ME

"About three in the afternoon Jesus cried out in a loud voice, "Eli, Eli,[a] lema sabachthani?" (which means "My God, my God, why have you forsaken me?")" Matthew 27:46

Once again, we come upon a prayer of Jesus that only he can pray. This prayer comes from the cross of Calvary. He has already been beaten, ridiculed, and spat upon. They have woven a crown of thorns and crushed them upon his head. Nails have been driven into his hands and feet. The sins of the world are upon him. One can only imagine how exhausted Jesus must have felt. There and then, he felt forsaken by his Father. What made him feel such? Only Jesus can know. But felt it he did. So, he cried, "Why have you forsaken me?"

While not in the same anguish as Jesus, the Psalmist often asked for God not to forsake him or the people of Israel. The Psalmist used different phrases to express the same concern.

"Do not forsake us."
"Do not rebuke me."
"How long O Lord?"
"Do not cast me off."

There are many other examples we can find in the Psalms.

We don't often think of even the possibility that God would forsake us. You might even say, "I don't think God will ever forsake me. I have too much faith, trust, and confidence in God. I would never think that." I would say you are right in your thinking. I don't think so either. But go deeper in this thought. What would we be asking if we ask God not to forsake us? Aren't we asking for an awareness of his closeness? Aren't we asking for God to be with us? Who doesn't want that! I know I do. Don't you?

PRAYER

Lord, do not forsake me. Make yourself ever so known to me. Make your presence so profound that I cannot help but acknowledge you. Make it so that if I were to deny it, creation around me would laugh out loud. Lord, I pray so earnestly for this.

I pray it for my church. While I know the church is the people, I pray that when we enter the building in which we worship that we will feel like we have to ask you to excuse us as we go to our seats. Make the people of my church rumble with excitement, as each time we gather we all have stories to tell of your presence in our lives.

Lord, encompass my pastor in your presence. Lord,

like Moses when he went into the tent of meeting, make it so obvious that he has been in your presence. Lord, not for his sake alone, but for our sake and those who may have come looking for your saving grace.

So be it, Lord. So be it.

DAY 6
MAY YOU NOT FAIL

"Simon, Simon, Satan has asked to sift all of you as wheat. But I have prayed for you, Simon, that your faith may not fail. And when you have turned back, strengthen your brothers." Luke 22:31-32

While we do not know the exact words of this prayer of Jesus, we do know the subject of his prayer: Peter's faith would not fail. Jesus asked his father to keep Peter from failing in his faith.

Some may say that Peter did fail. After all, he did betray Jesus during the arrest and trial of Jesus. I am not so sure Peter's faith truly failed during that time. I think Jesus knew Peter was going to deny him but that was not the failure. Jesus was more concerned that the denial would be so difficult on Peter that he would never return to the faith. This is why the last phrase of the prayer is important.

"...when you have turned back..."

Jesus knew Peter was going to deny him. The prayer was that Peter's faith would not fail him and that Peter would return, leading the disciples in the mission they were to be given.

Let's think about the first phrase as a model for our prayers: that our faith may not fail. Imagine if that were the prayer for the day.

Lord, help me that my faith may not fail.

Truly we do not know what tomorrow is going to bring. We do not know what struggles, devastations, or tragedies we are going to face. We may say that we would never abandon our faith in God. And, that might be true. However, this prayer isn't a question of your faithfulness, but a reliance on God's strength for that faithfulness. I, for one, know myself all too well. I may have a strong discipline and commitment, but I would never rely on my own strength to remain faithful to God. I need God. I need God to keep me faithful. So keep that prayer in mind.

Perhaps we could say this prayer for our spouse, our children, someone we know who may be struggling. You could even pray this prayer for your pastor or your fellow church members.

PRAYER

Lord, help me that my faith may not fail. Help me when I am in the face of temptation, in the face of tribulation, when I must decide on how to act - what to say, how to respond – do not let my faith fail. And Lord, if I make the wrong decision, if my actions deny you, please draw me back. Please lead me to return.

I pray this prayer for my church also. It is inevitable that we will have setbacks. Help us to know Lord, setbacks are not the end.

Be with my pastor especially. Let him rely on your strength, not his own. If, no, when he stumbles, pick him back up and put him back to his task of proclaiming the gospel.

I pray this in Jesus name, Amen.

DAY 7
STRENGTHEN YOUR BROTHERS

"Simon, Simon, Satan has asked to sift all of you as wheat. But I have prayed for you, Simon, that your faith may not fail. And when you have turned back, strengthen your brothers." Luke 22:31-32

Yesterday we looked at this prayer of Jesus. We mentioned that this is not a word by word copy of the prayer. Rather, Jesus tells Simon the subject of his prayer for Simon. We mentioned the phrase about unfailing faith. Today we will consider the second phrase,

"...strengthen your brothers."

What a very direct prayer for the work of Christians. Here, Jesus was praying for one person, Simon, who if the prayer was answered (we have no reason to think it wouldn't be or wasn't) many others would have their faith strengthened.

Every Christian is called to strengthen other Christians. It is our task as part of the body of Christ. We encourage, edify, and exhort one another. Often, we have the tendency to think those functions just happen in the life of the church. But what if we intentionally prayed for it to happen? What if it became a focus of our prayers? That is, we directly ask God to help us to strengthen others. I might even say the preface to such a prayer is that we ask God first to strengthen our faith, then we ask God to help us to strengthen the faith of others.

PRAYER

Lord, strengthen my faith. Make me stronger in you. Help me to strengthen the faith of my brothers and sisters in Christ. Give me the opportunity to give an encouraging word. Make me aware when one is struggling so that I may walk by their side.

Lord, strengthen the faith of my pastor. Help him to come to know you more and more. May you help him as he works to strengthen the faith of our church. May he be an encourager, an edifier. May the words he preaches be music to our souls, uplifting us, and propelling us forward in mission and ministry.

PrecisionFaith Break

I hope that you have been paying attention to the direction the prayers of Jesus take us. Praying with Jesus is powerful. It can literally change your prayers. I believe it can change us and the church.

PrecisionFaith uses a very precise method of discipleship. While the Holy Spirit is like the wind – coming and going – as God directs, being intentional in discipleship is important.

Praying with Jesus provides such a format. You could take these prayers, beginning at the first prayer and not move on to the second prayer until you are comfortable with the first.

For example: You spent however long it took learning to pray anywhere (Day 1). Then, and only then, would you move to praying blessings (Day 2). I would suggest once you became comfortable openly blessing someone; say like as you left their house from having coffee, then you would move to the revealing prayer (Day 3). The process of gaining confidence with each prayer is the signal to move to the next.

Consider this: Who taught you how to pray? From my experience in asking this question, the most common answer is no one. Unless a person had a parent that prayed in front them - something other than a meal blessing - people generally aren't taught how to pray. It's no wonder we think that praying means asking for somebody that is sick to get well. Or, when our world falls apart, we yell for God to help. Those are ways of praying, but they miss how we are taught to pray by Jesus' examples.

Just in these past seven days, we can see how different our prayers are from that of Jesus.

1. Praying anywhere.
2. Blessing others.
3. Thanking God for revealing himself.
4. Praying for God's will.
5. Asking God to not forsake us.
6. Asking God to help us not to fail.
7. Asking God to help us strengthen our brothers and sisters in Christ.

I want to encourage you to really consider your prayers with that of those of Jesus. How can you adjust your prayers? How can you shift your focus in your prayers to be like that of Jesus?

DAY 8
FORGIVE THEM

"Jesus said, "Father, forgive them, for they do not know what they are doing."" Luke 23:34

This is the second of three prayers that Jesus spoke from the cross. His persecutors had just led him through the streets. Stripped. Beaten. Whipped. He had been taunted. Forced to carry his own cross. Once at the site where he was to be crucified, they laid the cross on the ground and made Jesus lay down upon it. Then, they drove spikes through his hands and feet. As if that was not agonizing enough, then they raised the cross up placing it in the ground. His body would have shifted with all his weight bearing down upon the nails in his hands and his feet. Brutal.

Jesus was innocent. His only guilt was being who he had claimed - the Son of God. Jesus had every reason to hold them accountable. He was right. They were wrong. His actions, however, are nothing that we would have expected. "...forgive them..." Forgive them is what he said. Forgive them is what he prayed.

How powerful of a prayer! Imagine if we prayed this prayer. What if part of our prayer practice was to pray for the forgiveness of others? Perhaps we could pray for those who have wronged us? I am confident someone somewhere has wronged you in your life. Maybe you didn't think much about it. Maybe you just brushed it off. What if, however, you spent time reflecting over your life thinking about those who have wronged you. Then, pray for their forgiveness.

What an opportunity God has given us! For some, looking back doesn't require much. They can easily recall being wronged. For some, it was yesterday. Pray for their forgiveness.

Another approach to consider is to think beyond personal wrongs experienced. Instead, think about the sins of the world in general. Would it be worthy to consider praying for their forgiveness also? I want nothing more than to see people forgiven. It doesn't matter if their sin was committed against me or someone else. It may be that their sin is strictly between them and God. Nevertheless, my heart's desire is for them to be forgiven.

Do you think God wishes to forgive them, that it is his will for them to be forgiven? I believe God wants to forgive them. So, why not ask for it?

Since through this series we have been thinking about our church pastors and leaders in prayer, could you pray that God will forgive your pastor? It doesn't matter if you know he has sinned or not. Last I checked, no person is perfect. Pray for your pastor's forgiveness.

PRAYER

O Lord, I pray first for my own forgiveness. Forgive me of my failures, my sins. Forgive those also who have sinned against me [list them out; be specific].

Forgive those that have sinned against others [list them again if you know].

While I don't know their sins, forgive those who have sinned against you. Lord, I can think you long to forgive all people. So, I am asking for it just as you desire for it. Let people come to know your forgiveness. Forgive them.

Forgive my pastor for anything he may have done against you or anyone else. Maybe he isn't aware of it. Maybe he didn't mean to. Maybe he is struggling as many people are. I pray for his forgiveness, for his sake, and for those he leads.

Forgive us all, Lord. Forgive us so that we can know you better. Amen.

DAY 9
I GIVE MYSELF TO YOU

"Jesus called out with a loud voice, "Father, into your hands I commit my spirit." When he had said this, he breathed his last."
Luke 23:46

This is the third prayer from the cross. It is finished. The work of Christ is done. He has paid the sacrifice for the sins of the world. There isn't anything left for Jesus to do in this part of his mission by God. So, Christ does the only thing left to do. He gives his spirit to God.

Imagine with me that you have exhausted all your physical and emotional strength. You have given all you can to a dilemma. You don't know anything else to do. In fact, the only thing left to do is to give yourself, the problem, and the struggle to God.

I find it amazing that after all the struggle and effort, being at our last, the only thing left to do is to give it over to God. We see this step in life as the last resort.

We have done all we could, and this is all that is left. Ironically, giving it over to God is the best thing we could have ever done. It should have been our first resort. If we had only started there, rather than ended there?

While I don't believe Jesus ended there, I do believe we can learn about where we are to start from Jesus. What if we commended our lives to God today? What if we commended our families, our jobs, our problems, to God now instead of at our wit's end?

The implications of such a prayer is endless:
- at the start of the day
- at the start of a relationship
- at the start of a job
- at the first sign of trouble
- at the first indication of a disagreement
- as soon as we see a decision needs making

This list could go on endlessly.

If you have never commended yourself to God before, I want to ask you to do so today. Commend your life to God. Tell God that you are offering yourself to him. Maybe you have your own list of issues you are facing. Stop trying to do it on your own. Stop right now. Present them all to God. One-by-one give them over. Maybe it is a struggle with a child, a disagreement with a friend, it may even be an enemy. Give it to God.

Pray today asking that your children, your spouse, your friends, commend themselves to God. Pray that your pastor will commend his life, his ministry, his leadership to God. What better prayer can you pray for those you love? Which of the following prayer is best: Praying that they get a job or praying they give themselves to God? Praying they get well or praying they have a loving relationship with Jesus? Sure, there are lots of things that would be nice for our loved ones and we want those things for them, but one of the greatest prayers you can pray is that they would give themselves to God.

But, if you are going to say that prayer for someone else, it might be best to pray it for yourself first.

PRAYER

Father, I commend myself to you. I give myself and everything about me to you. My problems, my difficulties, even my victories and successes, they are yours.

I commend my church to you. Everything we have done and everything we shall do, I give to you.

I pray for my pastor. My prayer is that each day he offers himself to you for the sake of the gospel. Help him to lead us in spreading the good news.

In Jesus name I pray. Amen.

DAY 10
THANKS FOR LISTENING

"So they took away the stone. Then Jesus looked up and said, "Father, I thank you that you have heard me. I knew that you always hear me, but I said this for the benefit of the people standing here, that they may believe that you sent me."" John 11:41-42

Here also, we find a prayer that Jesus prayed that can only be prayed in its context. This prayer was prayed following the resurrection of Lazarus, a close friend of Jesus. Lazarus had died days before. The family of Lazarus had sent word to Jesus to tell Jesus Lazarus was ill. They expected Jesus to come right away and heal Lazarus. Jesus didn't however, and Lazarus died.

Jesus came to where Lazarus was days later. There was a conversation between Jesus and Mary as to why he had not returned right away. Mary told Jesus if he had been there, Lazarus wouldn't have died. Jesus had a different plan. He resurrected Lazarus. After calling forth Lazarus from the grave, he spoke this prayer.

Interesting is the reason for the prayer. Jesus said,

> "I have said this for the sake of the crowd standing here, so that they may believe that you sent me."

The purpose of praying this prayer was so that others may believe that God had sent Jesus.

While we can't pray this prayer in its context, we can learn from this prayer. We can focus on two key aspects of this prayer, once again, adapting them to our prayers as we learn to pray with Jesus.

Today we will focus on the first section of this prayer:

> "Father, I thank you that you have heard me. I knew that you always hear me…"

Have you ever simply thanked God for hearing you?

I had a mentor once that was a tremendous help and counselor to me. She would listen very attentively and provide guidance and wisdom. Sometimes it wasn't the words I wanted to hear, but I needed to hear them. As our paths separated, I thanked her for listening. Over the course of the years as we have contacted one another, I have often told her thank you.

Thanking God for listening is exactly what Jesus did. In fact, even though there was a reason for this prayer, it was really all Jesus said in this prayer. "Father, I thank you that you have heard me. I knew that you always hear me."

Today, thank God for listening. I would encourage you to let the subject of your payer today to be only about God listening. Just thank God for listening and tell him the confidence you have in that he has always heard you.

Now, as we have been doing these past several days, consider tweaking the focus of listening from yourself to your pastor. Thank God for listening to your pastor. Ask God to help your pastor to have confidence that God hears his prayers.

PRAYER

Lord, I thank you for listening to me. I know that you always hear me, and you are more ready to hear than I am to pray. But, when I come to you, you listen. Thank you.

I pray for my pastor also. I thank you for listening to my pastor. I pray that you will give him the confidence to know that you always hear him. Let him never have a doubt that you are listening.

I thank you again, Father. Amen.

DAY 11
SENT

"So they took away the stone. Then Jesus looked up and said, "Father, I thank you that you have heard me. I knew that you always hear me, but I said this for the benefit of the people standing here, that they may believe that you sent me."" John 11:41-42

As a pastor who has proclaimed the gospel in many different places across the world, I cannot tell you the number of times people have come up to me saying, "We are so thankful to God. He sent you to us."

As a counselor, I have had numerous individuals who I was working with through various experiences say to me, "There is no doubt, God put you in my path."

As a military chaplain, I have arrived at outposts, operating bases, and even on the battlefield, to have commanders and soldiers say, "Chap, you came out the right time. God must have known that we needed you."

Today, we want to focus on the last phrase of this

prayer,

"...so that they may believe that you sent me."

Jesus thanked his Father for hearing him. He knew God heard him, but he said it anyway so that those who heard him pray would know that God had sent him.

Jesus also knew he had been sent by his Father. He knew God had given him a mission to complete. He had been sent and he believed it.

We don't often think that we are sent, but we are. We are sent into the world to make disciples of Jesus Christ. Every person in the church, every person who considers themselves as a disciple of Christ, is sent to make disciples of others.

Maybe one of the church's difficulties today is that we don't believe we have been sent. Perhaps we no longer view ourselves as a missional agent sent by God to bring others to Christ. The Apostle Paul used words like ambassador and emissary to describe the church. Have we lost sight of those terms? It may be that we no longer believe the great commission. Or somehow, we don't believe it applies to us.

Listen, according to God's Word, we are sent. According to the teachings of Jesus, he sent us. Perhaps this is where we need to start in our praying with Jesus today. Perhaps we need to begin by asking God to help us to believe we are sent. Maybe we need to pray that God will rekindle that mission within us, to remind us we have a mission.

Once we have that realization that we are sent, and we believe it, then we can shift our prayers to those we are sent to. Then we can begin to pray that God will help those to whom we minister to realize that God has sent us to them so they can come to know the incredible experience of living within the Kingdom of God.

We have an incredible message. The song that states our message is "the sweetest ever that was heard" is correct. We have been given that message and God wants us to share it. But to share it, we must go. We must go to others. We must understand that the church we worship in was placed where it is so that it could tell that message to others in the community.

Can you pray that God will help us to pray that? Can you pray that your pastor believes in his calling? Can you pray that you, and your church, can have the mission burn brightly within them? What about those who will hear? Will you ask that God help them to know that you have been sent to provide them the greatest message known to humanity?

PRAYER

Father, help me to believe that you have sent me to tell others about the gospel of Jesus Christ.

Help my church to know that we have been established to share your love with our community. We are a missional church. We are not there for ourselves, but we are there to carry the message of hope to others. Help us to go.

Help my pastor to know and believe in his calling. Help him to know each day as he preaches and teaches that you sent him for this purpose.

Father, I pray for those who will hear the message proclaimed. Help them to know that it is your message. You gave it to me, my church, and my pastor, just for them; so that they may believe in you. So be it. Amen.

PrecisionFaith Break

We are going to take this PrecisionFaith Break a bit earlier this week. The next prayer of Jesus is a long prayer that will bring us to the conclusion of our twenty-one days praying with Jesus.

Over the last four days we have prayed for four new things:

1. Forgiveness of others.
2. Giving ourselves to God.
3. Thanking God for hearing us.
4. Help us to know we are sent and that others will know we are sent.

Except for thanking God for hearing us, the others might not be something you have heard prayed often. I know haven't, and only after learning it myself did I begin including them in my prayers. Sure, we ask forgiveness for ourselves, but not often for others.

Recall in the last PrecisionFaith break, I spoke of not moving on to a new prayer until you are comfortable and confident in the previous prayer(s). This can't be any more important than at this point.

If you cannot ask God to forgive others, then giving yourself to God might not be very appropriate. Our own forgiveness is tied to forgiving others (see the Lord's Prayer).

Our last prayer on being sent is critical if we are to understand this next prayer on Day 12. If we aren't ready to go for Jesus – to be sent – then we really aren't ready for the next prayer.

Take some time and think about your commitment to Jesus. If you haven't realized it yet, the prayers of Jesus are directly connected to the mission his Father gave him – the mission of offering eternal life to the world.

As a disciple of Jesus, we have received the mission of sharing that gift with others as well.

DAY 12
THE LONGEST PRAYER

"After Jesus said this, he looked toward heaven and prayed: "Father, the hour has come. Glorify your Son, that your Son may glorify you. For you granted him authority over all people that he might give eternal life to all those you have given him. Now this is eternal life: that they know you, the only true God, and Jesus Christ, whom you have sent. I have brought you glory on earth by finishing the work you gave me to do. And now, Father, glorify me in your presence with the glory I had with you before the world began.

"I have revealed you to those whom you gave me out of the world. They were yours; you gave them to me and they have obeyed your word. Now they know that everything you have given me comes from you. For I gave them the words you gave me and they accepted them. They knew with certainty that I came from you, and they believed that you sent me. I pray for them. I am not praying for the world, but for those you have given me, for they are yours. All I have is yours, and all you have is mine. And glory

has come to me through them. I will remain in the world no longer, but they are still in the world, and I am coming to you. Holy Father, protect them by the power of your name, the name you gave me, so that they may be one as we are one. While I was with them, I protected them and kept them safe by that name you gave me. None has been lost except the one doomed to destruction so that Scripture would be fulfilled.

"I am coming to you now, but I say these things while I am still in the world, so that they may have the full measure of my joy within them. I have given them your word and the world has hated them, for they are not of the world any more than I am of the world. My prayer is not that you take them out of the world but that you protect them from the evil one. They are not of the world, even as I am not of it. Sanctify them by the truth; your word is truth. As you sent me into the world, I have sent them into the world. For them I sanctify myself, that they too may be truly sanctified.

"My prayer is not for them alone. I pray also for those who will believe in me through their message, that all of them may be one, Father, just as you are in me and I am in you. May they also be in us so that the world may believe that you have sent me. I have given them the glory that you gave me, that they may be one as we are one— I in them and you in me—so that they may be brought to complete unity. Then the world will know that you sent me and have loved them even as you have loved me.

"Father, I want those you have given me to be with me where I am, and to see my glory, the glory you have given me because you loved me before the creation of the world.

"Righteous Father, though the world does not know you, I know you, and they know that you have sent me.""
John 17:1-25

This is the longest prayer we have of Jesus. It is spoken right before he is betrayed by Judas and arrested by the authorities under the motivation of the Jewish religious authorities. We could say that this was the farewell prayer for his disciples.

We will not deal with this prayer as a whole prayer. Rather, we will break it down over the course of the next six days. This will be the last prayer of Jesus in our journey together in this book in praying with Jesus. Hopefully, it will not be the end of your journey of praying with Jesus and this book has changed the way you pray. However, this prayer is a perfect transition point. In my view, it is the most powerful prayer of Jesus. As we shall discover over the next six days, it lays out the very mission of every Christian. And, if the prayer is followed, it is a never-ending process of sharing God's love until Christ returns.

Today simply contemplate upon this prayer. I am absolutely convinced if we took this prayer seriously, it would change us dramatically. You will see.

PRAYER

Father, I pray today that you will prepare me to receive what I can learn from this prayer of Jesus. Help me to receive what you want to teach me.

In the name of Jesus, I pray. Amen.

DAY 13
A PLACE TO GLORIFY YOU

"After Jesus said this, he looked toward heaven and prayed: "Father, the hour has come. Glorify your Son, that your Son may glorify you. For you granted him authority over all people that he might give eternal life to all those you have given him. Now this is eternal life: that they know you, the only true God, and Jesus Christ, whom you have sent. I have brought you glory on earth by finishing the work you gave me to do. And now, Father, glorify me in your presence with the glory I had with you before the world began." John 17:1-5

Jesus asked his Father to glorify him, not so he could feel good about himself, not so he could have a super-spiritual experience, but so that he could glorify the Father. This should be the single motive for us to want to grow in our faith. It should be the single motive of prayer itself - to glorify God. All that we do - no matter how complex or how simple - should be done in order to glorify our Father.

So how are we glorified? How do we ask God to glorify us? Well, if the request to be glorified is so that we can glorify our Father then our prayer should be that God put us in places that we can bring him glory. Can you imagine such a prayer? "Lord, put me somewhere today that I can bring you glory, that I can glorify you. Give me that opportunity." What an incredible prayer! And, this was the prayer that Jesus had prayed. This was the prayer of Jesus' life. It is all that he wanted to do.

But how do we glorify God? How did Jesus? Jesus said in this prayer that his method of glorifying God was by giving eternal life to others. This was his mission. This is what Jesus came to do. Further, Jesus defines eternal life as knowing the Father, the only true God, and Jesus Christ, who God had sent. That is the definition of eternal life. So, we glorify God every time we share that message. Every time we tell someone about the gift God has given to us all, we are glorifying God.

Our prayer has now expanded a bit: Lord, put me somewhere today that I can glorify you by telling others about eternal life. Now we are getting somewhere with praying with Jesus. Remember earlier in this book I mentioned we don't typically pray as Jesus prayed. Might we be getting closer to why we don't? Do you really want to tell someone else about Christ? You should. It is greatest way to bring glory to God. It is the greatest way to glorify his name. Sharing the gift of eternal life is the heart of the gospel. It is what the church was destined to do. It is what every Christian was purposed to do. It is the work we have been given. Jesus' work was to be the sacrifice through which we receive the gift of eternal life. Our work is to tell others about that gift.

So here is the prayer today. Pray it if you dare. But be careful, God will give you what you ask.

PRAYER

Lord, put me somewhere today that I can glorify you by telling others about eternal life. Give me the opportunity to share with them the message of knowing you, the only true God, and Jesus Christ, your Son whom you sent.

Put my church in a place to do the same. Give us every opportunity to glorify you through sharing the gospel.

Place upon my pastor, the undeniable joy of glorifying you every time he preaches.

This is our work. This is what you have given us to do - our mission. So be it. Amen.

DAY 14
GIVE ME THE WORDS

"I have revealed you to those whom you gave me out of the world. They were yours; you gave them to me and they have obeyed your word. Now they know that everything you have given me comes from you. For I gave them the words you gave me and they accepted them. They knew with certainty that I came from you, and they believed that you sent me. I pray for them. I am not praying for the world, but for those you have given me, for they are yours. All I have is yours, and all you have is mine. And glory has come to me through them. I will remain in the world no longer, but they are still in the world, and I am coming to you. Holy Father, protect them by the power of your name, the name you gave me, so that they may be one as we are one. While I was with them, I protected them and kept them safe by that name you gave me. None has been lost except the one doomed to destruction so that Scripture would be fulfilled." John 17:6-12

The problem with praying the previous prayer on Day 13 is that you must know what to say when the time comes. God will give you the opportunity to share the gospel. I suspect we are put in places to glorify God more often than we realize. But, when that time does come, and it will, we must be prepared to know what to say.

Now, there are several approaches to sharing the gospel. Many denominations and Christian organizations have created templates, pamphlets, tracks, etc. to share. While many of them are good and many people have come to Christ through them, I have always found that each opportunity is different and unique. Just as every congregation is different, so is each person. Just as a sermon created for a specific church at a specific time, so it is with people. The problem is, unlike a church, you never know what person you are going to have the opportunity to share the gift of eternal life with. This fact alone is the very reason we should pray today's prayer.

Jesus prayed,

"For I gave them the words you gave me and they accepted them."

Every sermon I have preached began with a prayer to the Father to give me the words to say. I ask God to tell me the right things to say in the right way. Not all sermons can be preached the same way to every congregation. I am dependent on God to give me the words and the way to say them so that they can be accepted by that specific congregation.

The same is true with every person that God sends us to. Because we do not know who that person will be, we should pray that God will give us the words he wants us to say, in the right time and in the right place with the right person. We should pray that God will keep the words of his gospel ever so near to our hearts, in our minds, and in our souls, so that when the opportunity comes, we are ready to share them. We will have been dwelling on them all day long. It is easy to talk with others about things that we think about all the time. The Gospel is no different.

PRAYER

Lord, I pray that you will give me the words today that I will need when you give me the opportunity to share the news about your grace and eternal life with someone. Place your gift ever so present on my mind that it is always before me. Prepare my heart, mind, and soul so that I am ready, willing, and able to tell of your goodness.

Do this with my church also. May you always be in the forefront of our thoughts.

Give our pastor the right words. Help him to know what to say so that we can accept them, hear them, and embrace them. Help him to have the words so that if someone who is listening that needs to hear of your love, can do so.

In Jesus name we pray. So be it. Amen.

DAY 15
LET THEM HEAR

"I have revealed you to those whom you gave me out of the world. They were yours; you gave them to me and they have obeyed your word. Now they know that everything you have given me comes from you. For I gave them the words you gave me and they accepted them. They knew with certainty that I came from you, and they believed that you sent me. I pray for them. I am not praying for the world, but for those you have given me, for they are yours. All I have is yours, and all you have is mine. And glory has come to me through them. I will remain in the world no longer, but they are still in the world, and I am coming to you. Holy Father, protect them by the power of your name, the name you gave me, so that they may be one as we are one. While I was with them, I protected them and kept them safe by that name you gave me. None has been lost except the one doomed to destruction so that Scripture would be fulfilled." John 17:6-12

Just as we must have the words to say, the people we share the gospel with must be ready to hear.

Each Sunday before I preach, and before any event I speak at, I pray that God will help the people hear. In the church I pastor, I walk up and down the aisles praying that God will fill their spirits with joy. I pray asking that God will help them grow in their faith. I pray that if someone doesn't know Jesus that God will open their hearts. I do this at every single event or service.

In this prayer Jesus said things like:

"…they have obeyed your word."

"Now they know that everything you have given me comes from you."

"For I gave them the words you gave me and they accepted them."

"They knew with certainty that I came from you…"

Jesus is glorifying God for the very fact that those to whom he had been sent received him. Jesus is giving God the credit.

If we are going to ask God to put us in places that allow us to share the gospel, if we are going to ask for the words to say, then we should be asking God to prepare the ears, the mind, the heart, and the soul of those to whom we speak. Just as we ask God to prepare us, we are asking God to prepare others. Of course, we are saying this type of prayer so that we can join Jesus in giving thanks to God that they listened. As a Christian, nothing should bring us joy like that of seeing someone coming to know Jesus. We should long for it. We should want to see it every day.

Paul states faith comes by hearing (Romans 10:17). The only way for a person to come to know the eternal life offered by God through Christ is by hearing. O Lord, open their ears. Let them hear.

PRAYER

Lord, I pray for those that you are going to send me to. I pray that you will open their ears. I pray that you will prepare their hearts, their souls, and their minds, so that they can hear the good news of Christ. May they know that the faith I share comes from you. Give them the power to obey your calling upon their heart.

I pray for every person in my church. I ask you will soften their hearts like freshly tilled fertile soil so they can receive your word like seeds sown by the master.

Help our pastor to hear you as well. May his ears be tuned to your voice, like a sheep that knows its shepherd.

In Jesus name I pray. So be it. Amen.

DAY 16
PROTECTION

"I am coming to you now, but I say these things while I am still in the world, so that they may have the full measure of my joy within them. I have given them your word and the world has hated them, for they are not of the world any more than I am of the world. My prayer is not that you take them out of the world but that you protect them from the evil one. They are not of the world, even as I am not of it. Sanctify them by the truth; your word is truth. As you sent me into the world, I have sent them into the world. For them I sanctify myself, that they too may be truly sanctified." John 17: 13-17

Let's face it. This world is hard. Being a faithful follower of Jesus Christ in this world is not easy. There are so many distractions, concerns, worries, and temptations. It is easy for a disciple of Christ to find themselves struggling in their faith. Many of them will fall away completely.

Now, this daily devotional isn't about whether we are "once saved always saved" or whether we can "fall from grace." This is not the point. The point has already been made - being a Christian can prove hard in this world. Jesus even says so.

I once read a book on the evangelism ministry of Billy Graham. Rev. Graham's organization spent enormous time and effort in trying to ensure new found Christians at his events were connected with local churches. They took this approach for the simple reason: Unless a person relates to a church, they will quickly fall away.

In the twenty-one years of my ministry, I have seen more people than I prefer to walk away from the church. Many of them returned to the lifestyles they lived before they accepted Christ.

Jesus prayed two things for those God had given him. First, he prayed for their protection. He prayed that God would protect them. Second, he prayed for their sanctification. He prayed they would continue to grow in the relationship with God.

My heart's desire is that everyone I share the good news of Christ with, and who receives it, will continue to grow in their faith. That's my prayer.

Today, we are praying that very thing. If, after all, we believe God will put us in places to share the gift of eternal life, give us the words to say, and prepare their hearts, then we can only anticipate seeing people come to the Lord. We should pray then, as Christ did, that God will protect them and help them to grow.

PRAYER

Father, I pray that the people whom you send me to that receive your word, accepting Jesus and the gift of eternal life, will be protected. Protect them from the world and its distractions, concerns, worries, and temptations. Help them to stay focused on you and you alone. Sanctify them. Continue their growth in their relationship with you.

Be with my church also. Let us not get distracted. Protect us from evil. Protect us from the works of the flesh that can destroy us so readily. Help us to grow in such a way that we will be a tremendous light to our community.

Protect our pastor. He is no different than anyone else. He is susceptible to distractions, concerns, worries, and temptations that pull him away from you. Cause him to grow in his faith. As our leader, may he always be a beacon of hope and promise.

In Jesus's name, Amen.

DAY 17
THOSE NOT YET

"My prayer is not for them alone. I pray also for those who will believe in me through their message, that all of them may be one, Father, just as you are in me and I am in you. May they also be in us so that the world may believe that you have sent me. I have given them the glory that you gave me, that they may be one as we are one— I in them and you in me—so that they may be brought to complete unity. Then the world will know that you sent me and have loved them even as you have loved me." John 17:20-23

Today, we will stretch our faith and prayers to new horizons. Have you ever tried to envision the people who will believe in Jesus Christ as a result of the work of those you have introduced to Jesus? Have you tried to see those not yet? Think of those who have yet to accept Jesus but one day will, not through you directly, but from the work of those you have led to Christ. That is really a far-reaching thought. Most of us do not think that way.

Imagine this: You tell a young person about Jesus. They accept Jesus and the gift of eternal life. They, in turn, will tell someone else. That person accepts Jesus. That person goes and tells another. You get the picture. This was the picture that appears in the prayer of Jesus.

"I pray also for those who will believe in me through their message" - the message of the disciples.

Jesus firmly believed, and expected, his disciples to tell other people about him and the message of eternal life. In fact, in the Gospel of Matthew, the very first disciples were told up front that making other disciples was part of the deal. Jesus said, "Follow me, and I will make you fish for people" (Matthew 4:19). So Jesus expected it and believed it would happen. Now he prayed for it.

I was at a Christian gathering a few years ago. Three young men introduced themselves to me and we begin talking about evangelism. One of the young men informed me that his friend, who was standing to his right, had led him to Christ. Then he nudged his other friend on the left and said, "And I led him to Christ."

I looked at this last young man and asked, "Well, who are you going to lead to Christ? It seems to be your turn."

The young man's eyes lit up as he began to tell me about someone he had been sharing the gospel with. Then, with absolute confidence he said, "It'll happen. I've asked God for it."

Guess what we are praying today? Are you getting excited? I am.

PRAYER

Lord, I pray for those who will believe in Jesus through the works of those I lead to Christ.

I pray Father for the next believers who will come after the ones currently in my church.

Prepare us Lord to teach and train our church, the current believers, to share their faith so that others can come to know you.

I pray for my pastor. May he teach and lead us in such a way that we see beyond the immediate and into the future not yet - that which is to come, those who are yet to believe.

O Lord, for your glory, and honor, and praise. Amen.

DAY 18
MAKE US ONE

"My prayer is not for them alone. I pray also for those who will believe in me through their message, that all of them may be one, Father, just as you are in me and I am in you. May they also be in us so that the world may believe that you have sent me. I have given them the glory that you gave me, that they may be one as we are one— I in them and you in me—so that they may be brought to complete unity. Then the world will know that you sent me and have loved them even as you have loved me.

Father, I want those you have given me to be with me where I am, and to see my glory, the glory you have given me because you loved me before the creation of the world.

Righteous Father, though the world does not know you, I know you, and they know that you have sent me. I have made you known to them, and will continue to make you known in order that the love you have for me may be in them and that I myself may be in them." John 17: 20-26

This is the final section of the longest prayer we have of Jesus. We considered yesterday how Jesus prayed for those yet to believe. Today we will look at the aspect of unity in Christ and the Father.

Jesus prays that just as he and his Father were one, so would those who believe. There are two aspects mentioned: the aspect of the glory of Jesus given to those you believe and the aspect of God's love.

Through this prayer we can't help but believe the glory Jesus spoke of was that of his relationship with the Father and that Jesus had done exactly what God had sent him to do. Isn't this what we all seek? Don't we want a relationship with God and to keep the teachings of God? Jesus is asking for those who will believe, but he also asks for God's love - the same love God had for Jesus. That is an incredible love. What's more! We have been given that love.

Here is what is interesting though. Our oneness with God is found in those two things - a relationship with God and God's love. And, having those two things are what Jesus says signifies the message we have been given to the world.

Praying for the church to have a relationship with God and to know God's love is quite a prayer. We are asking for the Father to strengthen our relationship with him. We are asking for us to know the love of God in a profound and significant way. Jesus never doubted that God loved him. He knew in very real and tangible ways that God loved him. This is what we are asking for the church. It is what we are asking for ourselves. So join today in praying this prayer:

PRAYER

Father, strengthen my relationship with you. Help me to know you ever so dearly each day. Reveal your love to me. Help me to know without a doubt that you love me. Push aside any questions or doubts that may creep into my mind. Remind me every day of your great love.

Help my church to know we have a living relationship with the creator of heaven and earth. That you love us unconditionally. Be with those who will believe as a result of our work. May they know the incredible and profound love and relationship that they have with you. Be with those who will believe as a result of their work.

Father, be with our pastor. Remind him of your great love and of his relationship he has with you.

In the name of the Father, the Son, and the Holy Spirit. Amen.

DAY 19
A LOOK BACK

Today I want us to simply look at the longest prayer of Jesus in its whole as we have adapted it to our prayers. Below is a simple list of what we prayed for in this prayer:

1. Put me in a place to glorify you by sharing the gift of eternal life.
2. Help me to know what to say and how to say it.
3. Help those whom you have sent me to share with to hear the words you have given me.
4. Protect those who will believe and help them grow in their relationship with you.
5. I pray for those who will believe from their work.
6. Make us all one with you and Jesus in relationship and in love.

Merely looking at this list, it becomes evident how powerful such a prayer is to pray. It certainly takes praying to a whole new level.

PRAYER

Father, thank you for what I have learned over these last seven days. Thank you for helping me to see my mission through the prayer of Jesus. He was certainly doing much more than just saying a prayer to you.

Give me the courage to pray this prayer every day of my life and the confidence to act upon it when you answer it.

In the holy name of my Lord, Amen.

PrecisionFaith Break

This is another summary break brought to you by PrecisionFaith.

The Longest Prayer that we just considered over the last seven days is different in the way we can approach it. This is not a prayer that you can pray the first day (Day 13) until you are comfortable and confident and then move to Day 14. The prayer isn't built that way.

If you ask God to put you somewhere to share the gift of eternal life, you better have the words. It might also be a good idea to have already asked for the person God puts in your path to be able to hear and receive that word. And, why wait to pray for their protection and growth, especially if we really believe God will give us what we ask for in such a prayer.

The Longest Prayer is best prayed fully.

I still can't get over how rarely we hear this kind of prayer in church. I suppose that is why I believe praying with Jesus can change us and the way we pray. The prayers of Jesus are just profound and shape us for the very purpose we were created. I can't help but recall the first call to discipleship Jesus ever gave:

> "Come, follow me," Jesus said, "and I will send you out to fish for people." Matthew 4:19

DAY 20
A LONG LOOK BACK

Today, like yesterday, I want us to look back. This time we are looking back at everything we have learned from praying with Jesus. This is a summary designed to let you see the trends and patterns of the prayer. This zoomed out view is very revealing. Let's take a look.

Day 1. We pray anywhere.

Day 2. We pray blessings.

Day 3. We thank our Father for revealing himself to us.

Day 4. We pray for God's will.

Day 5. We ask God not to forsake and make himself known.

Day 6. We pray that we will not fail.

Day 7. We pray that he helps us to strengthen our fellow Christians.

Day 8. We pray for forgiveness - our own and others.

Day 9. We give ourselves to God.

Day 10. We thank him for listening to us.

Day 11. We pray that he will help us believe that we are sent to share the gospel.

Day 12. This day was a contemplation on the longest prayer of Jesus as we prepared to study it.

Day 13. We ask God to put us in a place to glorify him by sharing the gift of eternal life.

Day 14. We ask for the words to say when the time came that we prayed for the day before.

Day 15. We ask that God would prepare the hearts, mind, and soul of those we share eternal life with.

Day 16. We prayed for the protection and growth of those who would believe through our sharing of the gospel. (Keep in mind we did this even before we ever shared the gospel. We are anticipating them. If we are obedient it will happen.)

Day 17. We prayed for those who would believe through the work of those we led to Jesus.

Day 18. We ask God to make us all one: One with God, one with Jesus, one with one another. (Remember, Jesus said the world would know through the relationship we have with God and his love.)

Day 19. On this day we looked back, recapping the longest prayer.

Do you see what I see? Do you see the incredible focus of Jesus on his mission, and our mission, and what we learned from his prayers in adapting them to our own?

Better yet, what is missing in these prayers in comparison to how we normally pray?

The prayers of Jesus are profoundly different. If we made them our own, the entire way we pray would change.

Even more, we would change. Our understanding and practice of discipleship and what it means to be a Christian would be transformed.

These are some serious and heavy prayers. This is the point of this book. It is what I pray that you gather from reading this book. The prayers of Jesus are deeply profound. I believe that Jesus wants our prayers to be just as profound.

Perhaps today you can use this list to shape your prayers. Go down the list - top to bottom. Reflect upon the prayer, or its practice, and pray them as one great prayer.

DAY 21
A FINAL PRAYER

Today is my turn to pray for you. The title of this devotional is *Jesus: 21 Days That Can Change the Way You Pray*. Day 21 is about you knowing the Father and the one he sent, Jesus.

I wrote this little devotional on the pretext that the reader would be a Christian already. That the reader would already have a relationship with Jesus and was interested in improving their prayer life.

The truth is, I don't know if you are a Christian already. I do not know if you have accepted God's gift of eternal life that he gave you through his son, Jesus. I just don't know. How remiss of me to ask you to pray these prayers without knowing. So, on day 21, I want to invite you to accept the message of eternal life.

I've been holding out on you a bit. My prayer before I wrote this book was that God would give me the opportunity to share eternal life with others (sound familiar). God gave me the opportunity by laying on my heart the desire to write this book (you probably do not realize how big of a step of faith this was for me).

As I wrote, I ask God to give me the right words.

I prayed that he would open your heart so you could hear.

I prayed that he would protect you and cause tremendous growth through your reading of this book.

I asked even that he would draw others through you. I absolutely believe that if you pray these prayers others will come to know Jesus through you.

I asked God to unite you in his love and in an incredible relationship with him and his son. I want that for you so much my heart hurts.

I prayed that God would reveal himself to you through this book.

I have prayed that he would forgive you, no matter who you are or what you have done.

I have asked him to strengthen you - to give you confidence.

I have even prayed that he will send you.

I have prayed that you will commend your life to him, especially to the sharing of eternal life. But, to share eternal life, you must receive it first. Jesus once said, "Freely you have received, freely give" (Matthew 10:8).

You must receive it first though.

So, if you haven't received eternal life from God, will you receive it now? Will you accept the gift God has given you? There is no magic prayer to pray. In fact, you don't have to say anything. Just receive it. Accept it in your heart. Believe that God sent his son, Jesus, for you.

The Apostle Paul wrote: "If you declare with your mouth, "Jesus is Lord," and believe in your heart that God raised him from the dead, you will be saved" (Romans 10:9).

Will you do that today? Will you say that right now? I pray that you will. I've already told you; I am praying even now for those that will believe because of you.

Maybe you are already a Christian. You have already accepted the incredible gift of eternal life. I am so glad. My prayer above is still the same. This is the neat thing about these prayers, you can say them for anyone. I pray, regardless of where you are in your relationship with God, that your prayer life has been changed by this book - by learning to pray with Jesus.

I realize this little devotional isn't earth-shattering material. It is fairly simple. Most of what Jesus taught is simple also. But, when we follow what he taught, when we pray as he prayed, when we do as he did, earth-shattering things happen.

So, I am praying that you have been blessed. This is what my Savior did, so I do unto you. I ask God to bless your life incredibly. I pray that whatever you do, you will have prosperity that leads to God. I pray blessings upon you, your church, and your pastor also.

May you know the Father and the Son. So be it. Amen.

ABOUT THE AUTHOR

Dr. Toby Lofton is the Founder of PrecisionFaith, a platform that helps clients to follow Jesus so that they can have a life of fulfillment, happiness, joy, and peace.

Toby considers himself a contemplative with deep monastic undertones. He is a pastor with a gift of preaching and teaching in simple ways that people understand.

A retired US Army Chaplain, Clinical Pastor, former professor of Biblical studies, and a pastor with over twenty years of experience, Toby loves to help others grow in their faith through discipleship that produces life-changing results. His key theme is discipleship.

When he is not preaching, teaching, or writing, he is passionate about health, fitness, and the outdoors.

He has no plans of retiring from following Jesus - ever!

Toby Lofton can be reached at info@precisionfaith.com.

Made in the USA
Middletown, DE
07 December 2022